DK 24 HOURS
Water Hole

LONDON, NEW YORK, MUNICH,
MELBOURNE, and DELHI

Written and edited by Zahavit Shalev
Senior designer Tory Gordon-Harris
Designer Sadie Thomas

DTP Designer Almudena Díaz
Picture researcher Sarah Pownell
Production Shivani Pandey
Jacket design Chris Drew
Jacket editor Carrie Love
Jacket copywriter Adam Powley

Publishing manager Susan Leonard
Managing art editor Clare Shedden

Consultant Ginger Mauney

With thanks to Lisa Magloff
for project development.

First American Edition, 2005

Published in the United States by
DK Publishing, Inc., 375 Hudson Street,
New York, New York 10014

05 06 07 08 09   10 9 8 7 6 5 4 3 2

A Cataloging-in-Publication record for
this book is available from the Library
of Congress.

ISBN 0-7566-1126-1

Color reproduction by Colourscan, Singapore
Printed and bound in China by L. Rex
Printing Co. Ltd.

Discover more at
www.dk.com

Welcome to the water hole

`6:00 am` Dawn

`9:00 am` Morning

Introduction   page 4
Dawn   page 6
Wading in   page 8
Poop!   page 10
Follow the herd   page 12

Morning   page 14
On the lookout   page 16
Tall stories   page 18
Early birds   page 20

You may not know this, but during the course of the day, the creatures of the grasslands perform many of the same tasks as you. They eat, sleep, rest, play, and keep themselves clean. Visit the water hole and see how everyone from dung beetles to elephants spends 24 hours.

a life-giving oasis in a parched landscape.

1:00 pm Afternoon

6:00 pm Dusk

10:00 pm Night

Afternoon	page 22	**Dusk**	page 32	**Night**	page 40
Baboon base camp	page 24	**Big cats**	page 34	**Midnight feast**	page 42
Tree for all	page 26	**Lion lifestyles**	page 36	**Chance meeting**	page 44
Life on the ground	page 28	**Carcass control**	page 38	**Glossary**	page 46
Meerkat madness	page 30			**Index**	page 48

Large, floppy ears cool the elephant down by letting the heat of its body escape.

Having few leaves means this tree can keep much of its moisture safely in its roots.

In *24 Hours* *Water Hole*, we will follow a day and night in the lives of the creatures that live near the water hole. Over the course of the day, we will return a number of times to the five animals on this page to see what they are doing.

Zebra

These horselike creatures stay close to water and form striped herds, so that predators cannot easily target individual animals.

Elephant

It takes a lot of food and water to keep an elephant going. The oldest herd member knows where the best supplies can be found.

Giraffe

Food is plentiful year-round for giraffes, since no one else can reach the leaves they feed on. This means they can breed at any time, so the males are always on the lookout for suitable females.

Introduction

Scale Use these guides to help you work out the size of the creatures you meet. They are based on children of about 3 ft 9 inches (115 cm) tall.

Wet and dry seasons

8:02 am During the brief but spectacular wet season, the lakes are brimming with water, and a lush, green layer of vegetation covers the ground.

8:02 am For the vast majority of the year, one or two water holes are the only source of water for miles around. The land dries out and cakes over.

Lion

With the king of beasts, life moves rapidly between feast and famine. During lean times lions get skinnier and skinnier as they go for days without anything to eat or drink.

Hawk

Opportunistic birds, African harrier hawks hunt at the water hole, lurk in trees looking for eggs and chicks, and walk along the ground in search of insects and fruit to snack on.

5

1 Elephant

The chilly night is over, but the sun hasn't come up yet. A troop of elephants gathers around the water hole. Occasionally, in the dry season, they can drain a water hole in one visit, leaving no water for anyone else.

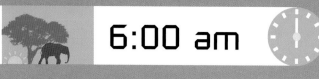

The **lion** and **lioness** lap at the water's edge following a night spent hunting and feasting. After a drink, they will doze the morning away.

The **zebras** and other herd animals drink once the predators are gone. They keep a lookout for one another just in case anyone else is still hungry.

The **giraffes** take their time at the water hole, munching leaves— something they do for at least 12 hours a day— while they wait to drink.

The **African harrier hawk** returns to her nest hidden in a craggy rock face far from the water hole. Her chicks cheep urgently for food.

The **elephant** digs in the soil for salt, an important part of its diet. Young elephants learn where the salt is buried from older members of the herd.

Elephants live in herds made of females and their children. The oldest and most **knowledgeable** elephant is in charge. She could be as old as 60. Males **leave** the herd at about 13 years old and sometimes form their own **bachelor** herd.

Pregnancy in elephants lasts almost two years, so babies don't come along that often.

The trunk is as useful to an elephant as your hands are to you.

Despite their **size** elephants are gentle...

Elephant skincare

If these elephants look a little dusty, that's because they are! After bathing, elephants suck dust into their trunks and then dump it all over their bodies. It acts as an insect repellent, and stops the sun from damaging their skin.

Bathtime for a baby elephant

10:02 am This baby elephant is feeling a bit uncertain about getting into the water and dithers hesitantly at the water's edge...

10:03 am A caring, motherly trunk reaches out. It first coaxes, and then gently pushes, the little elephant in.

10:25 am Once in the water, all fears are forgotten. Adults and baby play contentedly in the cool water.

...but these springboks **scramble** out of the way when they approach!

Broad feet help to spread an elephant's weight so it's very steady on its feet.

The area surrounding the water hole is patterned with paths the elephants have created as they travel between the water hole and the forested areas where they go to eat leaves.

Insects and other creatures disturbed by the elephants' heavy tread are swiftly snapped up by waiting birds.

Elephants walk at a **leisurely** 3 miles (5 km) per hour, but they per hour if they **need** to!

Elephants can communicate with each other over distances as far as 1½ miles (2.5 km). We can't hear these sounds, so it surprises us when many elephants suddenly arrive at the water hole at the same time.

can **run** at 25 miles (40 km)

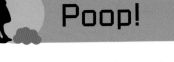
Recycling elephant dung

8:10 am Since it doesn't digest its food very efficiently, a lot of useful matter remains in the 220 pounds (100 kg) of dung produced by an **elephant** each day.

8:20 am First to arrive are **butterflies**. They cluster around the fresh dung and suck out the nutritious liquid.

10:00 am Birds eat the seeds contained in the dung, and pluck out undigested grass and straw to use in building their nests.

5:00 pm Dung **beetles** form the dung into small, compact balls. They determinedly roll these to their tunnels and lay eggs on them.

11:00 pm If what remains by now is damp enough, **mushrooms** may start to sprout from the dung pile. That means food for yet more animals.

There's safety in numbers for the members of a herd. If you're a strong healthy animal and a hungry lion appears while you're grazing, there's a good chance the unlucky victim will be someone else!

Most grazing animals drink at least once every day, so they can't stray far from the water hole. The tracks they make as they travel between feeding grounds and the water hole are etched into the landscape.

When food is scarce, male impalas have no energy to defend their territory or fight for females.

If attacked, this tranquil herd of impalas will **explode** into a chaotic frenzy of leaping to confuse their attackers.

Home on the plains

Peculiar-looking wildebeest wander over vast distances in search of grass and water.

8:00 am Zebras live in family groups. They graze together and groom one another by nibbling at each other's backs and manes.

8:35 am Two males rear up, kicking and biting each other. They are competing to head the group and breed with the females.

8:41 am Mothers are very close to their young. Relatively few zebra foals are killed by predators because the herd protects them well.

8:56 am Sensing danger, they scatter. Stripes make it harder for a predator to single out an individual.

1 Combretum tree   **2** Giraffe
3 Guinea fowl   **4** Zebra   **5** Springbok

Midmorning at the water hole and it's busy, but the animals line up patiently to wait their turn. Fights hardly ever break out because everyone knows the rules and makes way for the elephants.

14

The lions are still relaxing. They don't have to be constantly alert because, at the top of the food chain, there is no one to prey on them.

The zebras are milling around near the water. Their striped coats dazzle their enemies and may also help them cope with the extreme heat.

The giraffes interlock necks and struggle together but don't injure each other. This play-fighting between young males is called sparring.

In the branches of a tree, the harrier hawk looks for food. As well as small animals, she will eat palm nut husks if she can find them.

Dust baths are a fun and important part of the elephant's routine. The dust gives the elephant its familiar dusty look.

There's plenty of high drama low down. Smaller predators like hyenas and jackals win their prey more with daring than with muscle, while rodents and insects spend time both above and below ground.

Bat-eared foxes listen for insects beneath the soil and then snap them up.

Dung beetles collect animal droppings and take them home as food.

Termites live in enormous underground colonies and eat dead and rotting matter.

The pack can take on and bring down a large animal like a

Cape ground squirrels live underground where it's quite chilly. They dig for roots and bulbs, and come up to the surface to sunbathe.

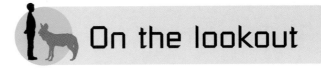
Spotted hyenas sometimes hunt alone but usually do better by cooperating and hunting in packs.

zebra or even a wildebeest.

Providing food for the family

10:29 am Black-backed jackals will eat most things. A jackal attacks a flock of sand grouse by the water's edge, making them scatter.

10:33 am Having caught and killed a bird, this jackal has to avoid having its prize snatched away by bigger predators on the way home.

10:40 am Three hungry cubs are waiting for their share back at the den. In a few months, they, too, will be out hunting for food.

It's great being tall. Giraffes can reach the juicy leaves at the top of the tree and see hungry lions a long way off. But there's at least one big disadvantage—it's a long way down to get a drink.

Responsible drinking

11:02 am It's safe to drink, so this giraffe starts to move its front legs apart.

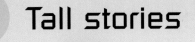

Giraffes roam in small herds of between three and 20 animals with no obvious leader.

This giraffe is taller than three tall men standing on each other's heads!

A giraffe has just **seven** bones in its neck, the same number as you.

Looking out for danger

Bending over is tricky, and getting up is even harder. A thirsty giraffe can spend hours making sure it's absolutely safe before quenching its thirst.

11:08 am Long legs move out some more and then the head goes down.

11:15 am One-way valves in the giraffe's neck stop blood from suddenly flooding its brain.

19

The birds that visit the water hole are extremely varied. They range from enormous ostriches to tiny oxpeckers, flesh-eating storks to insect-crunching hornbills, and group-loving guinea fowl to solitary storks.

Delicate and pretty they may be, but **lilac-breasted rollers** make a surprisingly harsh squawking sound!

Oxpeckers and giraffes form an **unlikely** partnership. The little birds keep the giraffes free of **ticks** and **fleas**.

Oxpeckers have been known to take advantage of their host by keeping the giraffe's insect wounds open so they can feed on its blood.

Ostriches are the largest birds in the world. They don't need much water, but they travel far in search of food even though they are unable to fly.

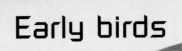

The beak is mostly hollow, so it is not as heavy and bulky as it looks.

Perched on top of an anthill, a marabou stork surveys the area. The thousands of ants living here have nothing to fear—the stork is only interested in eating meat.

This bush cricket's defense is the **stink** it gives off when attacked.

This **yellow-billed hornbill** uses its beak to grab and eat seeds and insects—including spiders and scorpions—from the ground.

Guinea fowl live in large flocks. By day, they peck at the ground in search of food. At dusk, their cackle can be heard as they settle for the night

In many parts of the world, people keep guinea fowl so they can eat them.

1 Gemsbok   2 Springbok

I t's the hottest time of the day, and the water hole resembles a swimming pool. Animals wade into the water and bathe, just passing the time until the temperature cools down.

Lion cubs scramble playfully over the **lioness**. They are practicing the skills they will use when they come to hunt as adults.

The **zebras** spend calm hours grazing at the dry, yellowish grass. Their diet consists almost entirely of grass with a few leaves and buds.

One of the **giraffes** crunches some bones. Giraffes have very tough mouths and tongues and like chewing on bones and thorns.

Soaring high above the water hole, the **harrier hawk** seems to be tossed around by currents of air, but her flight is actually very stable.

The **elephant** plays in the water to keep cool. Its trunk can hold 2½ gallons (10 liters) of water and is a powerful water pistol!

A **combretum** tree provides more than **shade**— its leaves, flowers, seeds, and roots are a baboon **banquet!** Baboons also eat whatever wanders by. Insects, birds, lizards, and

The adults sit quietly—it is really too hot to be rushing around.

small animals should beware if they don't want to become somebody's **lunch**.

Babies catch a ride on their mothers' backs.

24

Young baboons playfully chase one another up the branches of a tree, and scamper around the trunk.

One of the gang

Being a baboon means doing everything together. Baboon gangs sleep in the same tree, and spend their days nearby looking for food, and drinking at the water hole.

During a friendly grooming session, the baboon doing the grooming gets to eat all the **juicy** bugs it finds!

During grooming, baboons lick each other. They love the salty taste.

25

Sociable weaver birds build enormous nests. Each bird has its own "apartment."

The relatively few trees dotting the landscape have very deep roots that enable them to survive long periods with no rain. Their leaves and fruit provide food for a variety of insects, birds, and small animals.

Black mambas can move as fast as you can run. And their venom is deadly.

Tree for all

About 40 baboons sleep at this baboon base camp and spend the day on the ground nearby.

Combretum trees can grow very large. Rhinos love to munch on the young leaves. As the tree grows older, deep cracks form in the bark, which will provide homes for many small creatures.

Clever killers

Boomslangs climb trees and slither between branches to catch lizards and even birds. As they chew their prey, they inject a lethal poison into it.

Skinks scuttle around looking for spiders and insects to eat. If attacked, a skink can shed its tail in order to make a quick getaway.

This mother **scorpion** carries her babies on her back. Over time, their exoskeletons (bony coverings) will gradually darken and harden.

Unusually for an owl, the **pearl-spotted owlet** often hunts by day. Despite its small size, it is very strong and isn't afraid to attack prey bigger than itself.

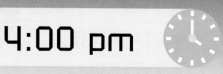

Warthogs normally live in burrows that have been dug by other animals.

The dusty earth looks uninviting, but many insects and reptiles find somewhere to live and a plentiful supply of food on or just below the ground. When the heat gets unbearable, they sit it out underground or in water and wait for cooler days.

Two pairs of bumpy "warts" between eyes and tusks give this peculiar-looking animal its name.

Impressive tusks are used for defense against lions and leopards. The lower set is very sharp.

Like their piggy cooling wallow

Life on the ground

Wet and dry survival strategies

Bullfrogs live underground during very dry periods so as not to dry out.

The forked tongue of the **rock monitor lizard** has no taste buds, but it can detect nearby prey by picking up scent particles in the air.

Rhinoceros beetles can carry 100 times their own weight, which makes them the strongest animals on Earth.

During very dry weather, female **leopard tortoises** will urinate on the ground to make it soft enough to bury their eggs.

Terrapins are turtles that live in water. They start life eating insects, but later turn to underwater plants and seaweed.

The most remarkable feature of the flap-necked chameleon is its tongue. The same length as the chameleon's body, it is spring-loaded and also equipped with a sucker. Needless to say, it is remarkably effective at snatching and gobbling up insects.

relatives, warthogs **adore** a in a muddy pool.

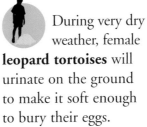

29

At sunrise, the whole mob emerges from their chilly burrow to warm up!

Sun-loving meerkats live in vast **underground** dens. Each member of the **mob** has a job. Baby-sitters in the den watch over the little ones, sentries outside keep a lookout for **danger**, hunters find food, and teachers **train** young meerkats to hunt.

Cooperation is the name of the game in a meerkat mob. Hunters always bring their food home to share......

Look out!

Sentries cheep or cluck if they sense danger, and bark or growl more alarmingly if a hawk or jackal approaches. Everyone instantly dives for cover.

At the **lookout post**, sentries perch on their hind legs, using their **tails** for balance.

Meerkat munchies

 Powerful front claws make digging up **beetles** a snap!

Worms, along with beetles, spiders, and other bugs, are an important part of the meerkat diet.

 Scorpions are gulped down before they can bite. Or perhaps meerkats are immune to venom.

Bolt-holes mean meerkats can make a swift exit if danger looms.

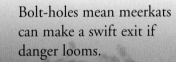

1 Leopard   2 Lion

Dusk descends quickly at the water hole. The large predators such as lions and leopards perk up as the temperature cools down. A pride of lions sharpen their claws on a convenient tree trunk.

The **lion** is the only adult male lion in the pride. He marks his territory with urine to warn other lions to stay off his turf.

The **zebras** head for the clearing where they will spend the night. They won't go farther than 7 miles (12 km) from the water hole.

This **giraffe** is still feeding on leaves as the sun sets. Male giraffes are taller than females so they don't compete for the same leaves.

Hovering under a sociable weavers' nest and using a leg to investigate, the **harrier hawk** looks for eggs or chicks to eat.

The **elephant's** trunk reaches out and expertly strips trees of leaves and branches. An incredible 50,000 muscles make it a very precise tool.

Roaring, not purring

Cheetahs are built for speed, not strength, so they don't always manage to keep their prey once they have caught it.

Caracals mostly eat birds and mice. They can spring as high as 10 ft (3 m) into the air to swipe and grab at birds as they fly past.

Lions are the most sociable of the big cats. They live in groups, known as prides, whose members cooperate by hunting together.

From its vantage point up a tree, a **leopard** quietly locates its victim and suddenly drops down for the kill.

Servals usually hunt at dusk, leaping up high and whacking their prey with their forepaws.

Most cats, with the exception of lions, live and hunt alone. They stalk their prey by silently creeping around close to the ground and then suddenly pouncing. Pinning their victim down, they strangle it, finishing the job with a lethal bite to the windpipe to cut off its breathing.

Cheetahs are the **fastest** animals on Earth. They can run at 62 miles (100 km) per hour but only for

Once a leopard has caught its prey, it drags it up a tree. A hungry leopard eats there, away from scavenging jackals and hyenas. If it's not hungry, the meat is hidden away for later.

20 seconds at a time.

The cheetah's long tail helps it make sudden sharp turns while giving chase.

Cats' eyes work very well at night. Cats see as clearly by starlight as a human sees by daylight.

After a kill, lions gobble down their food and then spend a day or so on a long after-dinner doze. They can afford to do this because no other animal dares to attack a lion, and anyway, it's a good way to pass the time between meals...

The job of the oldest male is to guard the pride.

The core of the pride are the 4–6 related lionesses who give birth at around the same time and care for each other's cubs.

Fresh meat for dinner

8:03 am After many hours in wait, a lioness selects her target—one of the weaker kudus in the herd.

8:04 am She runs powerfully toward her victim. Panicking, the kudu notices too late and tries to flee.

8:05 am The lioness grabs the kudu. With a swipe at the legs and a bite to the spine, this kudu stands no chance.

8:15 am Other lions join the hunter and dig in to a big meal. The next few hours will be spent digesting!

Yawnnnn

When a lion yawns, rather than roars, you can see its enormous tongue. It is covered with hard bumps, rough enough to scrape meat from bones.

Lion cubs in the lair greet their mother excitedly on her return from a hunting trip. She leads them to her kill for a share of the meat.

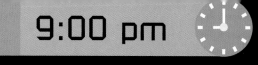

Lions prefer fresh meat, but the leftovers don't just lie around decomposing. Scavengers polish them off. They'll eat anything that was once alive! As nature's garbage collectors and recyclers, they consume every last scrap of flesh and bone left by the big hunters.

The lion in the pride hangs back. He watches distance and then barges

Lionesses drink after a kill. Although they are the hunters and actually do all the hard work, the males of the pride usually eat first, followed by the lionesses, and then the cubs.

the **action** lazily from a

in to get the first bite!

This wildebeest will be just a skeleton within a few hours. Only a very hungry hyena would devour the bones.

Enough for everybody

9:14 pm High in the sky, **African white-backed vultures** use their amazing eyesight to spot the dead wildebeest far below. They make cackling and hissing sounds as they feast.

9:21 pm Hyenas arrive as the vultures leave. They bolt their food down, eating as much as a third of their own body weight, before trotting off across the plains.

9:25 pm Lappet-faced **vultures** scare the hyenas away. By ripping through the wildebeest's hide with their hooked beaks, they make it easier for other scavengers to feed next.

9:46 pm Black-backed **jackals** eat quickly, expecting to be pushed out of the way when larger scavengers arrive. Back in their den, they regurgitate some food for their young.

9:50 pm Marabou storks pick at the flesh of the wildebeest. They are bald so there are no feathers to get messy when they poke their heads into the rotting carcass.

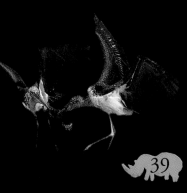

10:00 pm

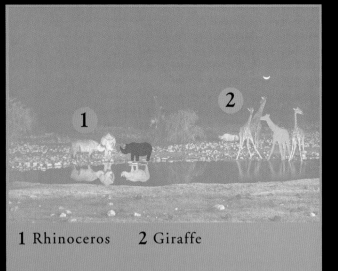

1 Rhinoceros   **2** Giraffe

Late at night the rustling of the undergrowth signals the arrival of rhinos and giraffes. Many other large animals, including elephants and lions, also come to drink during the cool hours of darkness.

The **lions** tear into an unfortunate impala. They eat as much as they can, since it may be another couple of days before their next kill.

The **zebras** huddle together at night. They lie down to sleep, but there are always some members of the herd awake, alert for danger.

The **giraffes** look wide awake. They bend their heads back against their bodies and sleep deeply for just a few minutes each night.

The **harrier hawk** spends some of the night in her nest, but also goes out hunting when her unsuspecting prey is resting.

The **elephant** needs around 50 gallons (200 liters) of water every day. To get its fill, the elephant spends much of the night drinking.

By day, colonies of fruit bats dangle **upside down** in trees.

This spotted eagle owl has excellent hearing. It can hunt in almost total darkness.

Predators,

whether large or small, usually favor nighttime for hunting. It's less tiring to give chase during the cool night, and prey might be asleep, so there's also the advantage of that element of surprise...

Black-backed jackals are determined hunters but will take advantage of any opportunity to scavenge a meal.

At night, they swarm out squeaking and whistling in search of fruit to eat.

Owls see well by day and night, but they have to swivel their heads because they can't move their eyeballs.

An unfortunate mouse barely has time to realize what's happening. This barn owl suddenly and silently grabs and kills it, swallowing it whole—fur, bones, and all. In a few hours, the owl will produce a pellet from its mouth containing the parts it is unable to digest.

 **Nightjars** feed on insects, literally grabbing them as they fly by.

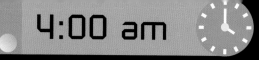
Black rhinos have small eyes and poor eyesight but very sensitive hearing and smell. They tend to spend the day resting in the shade and feed at night. When two meet each other at a water hole, they huff and snort, kick up the dust, and then generally ignore each other.

Lions sometimes attack small, adolescent black rhinos, but they don't usually go for adults like this one.

There's just not enough vegetation available to support many black rhinos, so each animal lives alone, marking out its territory with urine and dung to keep others away. A pair of rhinos are usually a mating couple who will stay together for a few days, or a mother and her calf.

Giraffes and elephants are often at the water hole in the middle of the night. They sleep far less than humans— about five hours out of 24— and spend almost all of their waking hours eating. Elephants are particularly frequent visitors, since they need to drink as much as 50 gallons (200 liters) a day.

The hooked lip of the black rhino is useful for pulling leafy branches into its mouth.

From dawn to dusk

Here are many of the creatures

Elephant · Zebra · Impala · Giraffe · Hornbill · Oxpeckers · Hyena · Ostrich

Glossary

Here are the meanings of some of the important words you will come across as you learn about the animals and birds that visit the water hole.

ADOLESCENT An animal that is no longer a baby, but isn't yet a full-grown adult capable of mating.

BACHELOR A male animal that does not have a female to mate with during the mating season.

BURROW A hole in the ground dug by animals so that they can live or hide in it.

CARCASS The dead body of an animal.

DUNG The waste matter produced by an animal.

EXOSKELETON The hard covering that some animals and insects

FLOCK A group of birds that live and fly together.

GRAZE To feed on grass or other green plants.

GROOMING The way that animals keep their fur and skin clean and free of insects.

HERD A group of animals, such as zebra or kudu.

INSECT REPELLENT A substance whose smell or taste keeps insects away.

MATING The way in which a male and a female animal come together to produce young.

MOB A group of meerkats

PACK The name for a group of jackals or hyenas that live together.

PELLET A ball of bones and feathers spat out by an owl some time after swallowing its prey.

PREDATOR The name for an animal that hunts, kills, and eats other animals.

PREY The animal that a predator hunts, kills, and eats.

PRIDE The name for a group of lions that live together.

REGURGITATE To bring food back out of the stomach to chew it again or feed it to someone else

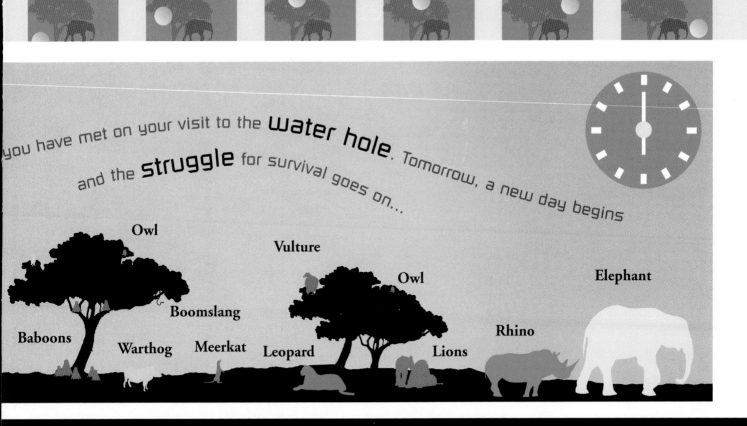

you have met on your visit to the **water hole**. Tomorrow, a new day begins and the **struggle** for survival goes on...

Owl
Vulture
Owl
Elephant
Boomslang
Rhino
Baboons
Warthog
Meerkat
Leopard
Lions

RODENT Animals such as squirrels or beavers that have strong teeth for chewing.

SCAVENGER An animal that eats dead animals but doesn't kill them itself.

SENTRIES Guards who warn the rest of the pack that danger is approaching.

SPARRING Playful fighting between young male giraffes that doesn't aim to cause actual injury.

STALKING Following an animal silently in order to launch a surprise attack.

VENOM The poison that scorpions and snakes inject into their attackers by biting or stinging.

Picture credits

Index

African harrier hawk *see* Hawk

Baboon 24-25, 27

Bat-eared fox 16

Bathing 9, 15

Beetle 31

Black-backed jackal *see* Jackal

Black mamba 26

Boomslang 27

Bullfrog 29

Bush cricket 21

Cape ground squirrel 16

Caracal 34

Cheetah 34-35

Combretum *see* Tree

Cooling down 3, 15, 22, 23, 28-29

Drinking 2, 7, 12, 18-19, 38

Dung 11

Dung beetle 11, 16

Elephant 2-3, 4, 6-7, 8-9, 10-11, 14-15, 23, 33, 41, 45

Flap-necked chameleon 29

Fruit bat 42-43

Gemsbok 22

Giraffe 5, 7, 14-15, 18-19, 23, 33, 40-41, 45

Grooming 25

Guinea fowl 21

Harrier hawk *see* Hawk

Hawk 5, 7, 14-15, 23, 33, 41

Hyena 16-17, 39

Impala 12

Jackal 17, 39, 42

Leopard 32, 34-35

Leopard tortoise 29

Lilac-breasted roller bird 20

Lion 5, 7, 12, 14-15, 23, 32, 33, 34, 36-37, 38-39, 41, 44

Marabou stork 21, 39

Meerkat 30-31

Nightjar 43

Ostrich 20

Owl 42-43

Oxpecker 20

Pearl-spotted owlet 27

Rhinoceros 40, 44-45

Rhinoceros beetle 29

Rock monitor lizard 29

Scorpion 27, 31

Serval 34

Skink 27

Springbok 9, 22

Termite 16

Terrapin 29

Tree 3, 24, 26-27

Vulture 39

Warthog 28

Water 2, 5, 6, 9, 29

Weaver bird 26, 33

Wildebeest 13, 38-39

Worm 31

Yellow-billed hornbill 21

Zebra 4, 7, 13, 14-15, 23, 33, 41